Ministero per i Beni e le Attività Culturali
Soprintendenza speciale per i beni archeologici di Roma

# ·roman·forum·
# ·palatine·
# ·colosseum·
## guide

**Electa**

*Editorial Coordination*
**Cristina Garbagna**

*Graphic Coordination*
**Angelo Galiotto**

*Graphic Design*
**Tassinari/Vetta** Leonardo Sonnoli
with Alessandro Panichi

*Page Layout and Editing*
**in.pagina srl**, Mestre-Venezia

*Edited by*
**Claudia Costantino**

*Translation*
**Richard Sadleir**

Reprint 2013
First edition 2008

© Ministero per i Beni
e le Attività Culturali
Soprintendenza speciale
per i beni archeologici di Roma

An editorial production by
Mondadori Electa S.p.A., Milan

www.electaweb.com

# Contents

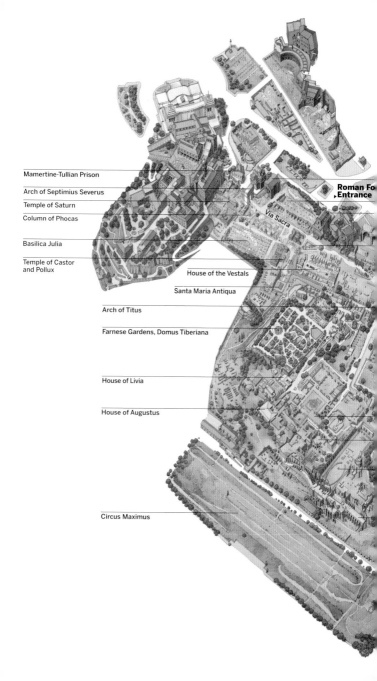

Mamertine-Tullian Prison

Arch of Septimius Severus

Temple of Saturn

Column of Phocas

Basilica Julia

Temple of Castor and Pollux

**Roman Forum Entrance**

Via Sacra

House of the Vestals

Santa Maria Antiqua

Arch of Titus

Farnese Gardens, Domus Tiberiana

House of Livia

House of Augustus

Circus Maximus

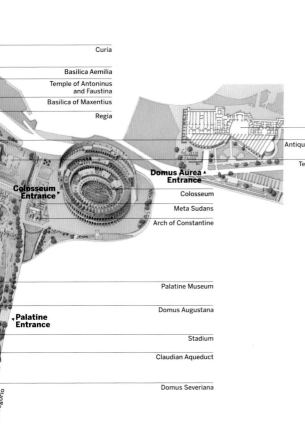

Curia

Basilica Aemilia

Temple of Antoninus
and Faustina

Basilica of Maxentius

Regia

Domus Aurea

Antiquarium Forense

Temple of Venus
and Rome

**Domus Aurea ▲
Entrance**

**Colosseum
Entrance** ▾

Colosseum

Meta Sudans

Arch of Constantine

Palatine Museum

Domus Augustana

▾**Palatine
Entrance**

Stadium

Claudian Aqueduct

Domus Severiana

Via di San Gregorio

# The Roman
# Forum

# The Roman Forum

In the monarchical period, this area was a marshy valley where the residents of the hills buried their dead. The Etruscan dynasty of the Tarquins paved it and used it as a public space. They drained it by channeling the local stream, the Velabrum, into the Cloaca Maxima.

In the sixth century BC the Romans built the Comitia which, together with the Curia Hostilia, became a meeting place for citizens, senators and magistrates. They also built the city's most ancient temples, dedicated to Saturn, Vulcan, Mars and Vesta.

The second half of the fifth century BC was a dark period for Rome and the Forum. Construction began again after the city was burnt by the Gauls (390 BC), but a more deliberate policy of building on a monumental scale was begun after the Punic wars (late third-early second century BC), when Rome came to dominate the whole of the Mediterranean.

The city's increased political power and the multiplication of contacts called for a new kind of urban design and architecture. Large buildings were erected for business and legal activities (the basilicas) and the shrines were rebuilt.

In the mid-first century BC, Caesar built his Forum by demolishing the Comitia and rebuilding the Curia. Augustus then built the temple to the deified Caesar on the east side. With the construction of the various Imperial Forums, the Roman Forum remained the city's symbolic center but lost its true political function, becoming the place where the emperors were deified after his death.

Apart from repeated restoration work, the last monumental

General view of the Forum
from the Capitol

The *Curia Iulia* with, in the foreground,
the base of the *Decennalia*

project was that of Maxentius in the early fourth century AD. Then followed the slow decline of the Forum and of Rome itself.

## The North Side

From Largo Romolo e Remo a flight of steps leads down to the level of the Via Sacra, which ran from east to west across the Forum and was used for religious and triumphal processions. As you go towards the Capitol, on the right you will find the **Basilica Aemilia**. Founded by a member of the *gens* (or clan) *Aemilia*, it dates from republican times, though its present appearance is the result of extensive restoration under the empire. Like the Basilica Julia opposite, it was used for administering justice and in bad weather housed all the activities normally conducted in the square.

On the side towards the Forum, with the entrances to the basilica, are some architectural fragments of the portico that Augustus dedicated to Caius and Lucius Caesar, his designated successors. You can also see the *tabernae* of the *argentarii* (money-lenders).

On the north-west corner stand the Comitia, the Curia and the Rostra. The republican Comitia formed a circular space surrounded by steps and used for public meetings. Little remains of it because Caesar occupied the site with his **Curia Iulia**. Next to the Comitia was the more ancient Curia, where the Senate met. The large brick building is the *Curia Iulia*, converted to a church in the seventh century. Two reliefs, the *plutei* of Trajan, are now in the Curia, though they once formed part of a monument in the Forum depicting the destruction of the registers of debts granted by Trajan and the institution of assistance for poor families. Both are set in the south-east sector of the Forum.

Also important in the city's political life was the podium used by magistrates, the Rostra (so called because they were adorned with the rostra or prows of the ships defeated at Antium in 338 BC), next to the arch of Septimius Severus. The remains date from Augustus's restoration of the structure.

Opposite the Curia is the *Lapis Niger*, an area of black marble paving surrounded by a balustrade, identified as the point where Romulus was killed, or vanished into heaven. The Volcanal (shrine of Vulcan) is also here. Excavations below this part of the paving have revealed the remains of a small temple consisting of an altar, the base of a statue and a stone with an inscription in archaic Latin (sixth century BC). It can be interpreted as a sacred law. This was clearly an ancient sacred precinct, dedicated to Vulcan, associated with the cult of the first king of Rome.

### The West Side

The Via Sacra continues through the **Arch of Septimius Severus**, a marble triumphal arch with three bays erected in AD 203 to celebrate victory over the Parthians. The attic bears a dedication to Septimius Severus and his son Caracalla. The decoration is very rich (with Victories bearing trophies, personifications of the seasons, river gods), but the most original part is the four panels showing the main phases of the military campaigns. The celebration of the emperor was completed by a bronze quadriga (four-horse chariot) surmounting the arch. Near the south pillar is a circular brick structure called the *Mundus* or *Umbilicus Urbis*: it was considered the center of Rome and a point of contact with the world of the dead.

This side is occupied by various shrines, such as the Temple of Concord, built by Camillus to mark the end of the conflicts between patricians and plebeians. Today only the plinth remains in situ, but the architectural decoration preserved in the *Tabularium* testifies to the importance of the shrine, where the Senate often met and where Tiberius placed the Greek originals of the works he brought to Rome. Next to it is the Temple of Vespasian and Titus, built by Domitian for his deified father and brother. Three Corinthian columns, the lintel and part of the inscription can still be seen. Also on the slopes of the Capitol is a building with a

The Arch of Septimius Severus

The Temple of Saturn viewed
from the Capitol

plan in the form of an obtuse angle, with eight rooms set in its sides. The inscription on the entablature identifies it as the Portico of the *Dei Consentes*, built in the Flavian period over an earlier republican shrine. The rooms behind once contained statues of the twelve *Dei Consentes*, the supreme divine pantheon.

On the south-west corner rise the slender columns of the **Temple of Saturn**, which replaced the god's original shrine, the *Ara Saturni*, visible under a roof opposite the steps. The remains of the temple date from the late third century AD, except for the plinth and the avant-corps, which are from late republican times. The avant-corps of the temple was hollow because it housed the aerarium, the treasure of the state. The base of a column opposite is all that remains of the *Miliarium Aureum*, a column erected by Augustus to mark the point where all the roads of empire converged.

### The Central Square

In the central area are some late honorary monuments: the column of the Byzantine emperor Phocas, the last monument added to the Forum (AD 608), and seven columns erected under the Lower Empire on the south side of the square. To the east of the Column of Phocas, set in the paving, there is a large inscription commemorating the curator of the paving in the Augustan period, Lucius Naevius Surdinus.

The Romans' three sacred trees (fig, olive and vine), which Pliny the Elder tells us grew in the center of the square, replaced the *Ficus Ruminalis*, the wild fig sacred to the god Faunus, in the imperial period. They have been replanted in the zone in front of the Rostra.

In the middle is an area set on a lower level, the *Lacus Curtius*, which remained a marsh until the time of Augustus. It was then reclaimed by sinking a well. Curtius is said to have been a Sabine leader who fell with his horse into the *lacus*. He appears on the late republican relief in the vicinity. But Livy derives the name from the consul Caius Curtius who, in the

The three surviving Corinthian columns
of the Temple of Castor and Pollux

mid-fifth century BC enclosed an area struck by lightning. The east side of the Forum is closed by the Temple of the Deified Julius, built by Augustus in 29 BC when Caesar was deified after his death. Today we can still see the plinth and the remains of an altar marking where Caesar was cremated. On the south side of the temple are the fragmentary remains of a triumphal arch erected by Augustus to mark his victory over Mark Antony. The *rostra* (prows) of the ships defeated at Actium were placed on the *Rostra ad Divi Iulii* facing the temple. A second Augustan arch, set symmetrically opposite the former on the north side, commemorated his victory over the Parthians. On the same axis as this, to stress the continuity of Roman dominion over the East, Septimius Severus then built the arch marking his victory over the Parthians.

### The South Side

Between the Temple of Saturn and the Temple of Castor and Pollux stands the **Basilica Julia**, begun by Caesar and completed by Augustus on the site of the republican Basilica Sempronia, which in turn was built on the house of Scipio Africanus. Between the Basilica Julia and the Temple of Castor and Pollux is the *Vicus Tuscus*, a street which took its name from the Etruscan quarter in the nearby Velabrum district. Shops flanked the *Vicus* and a large hall belonging to a Domitian complex, partly absorbed in the sixth century into the church of Santa Maria Antiqua. Recently the brick hall has been identified as the Temple of Minerva, in which Hadrian founded the *Athenaeum* and where heirs to the throne were educated.

To the south are the remains of the *Horrea Agrippiana*, warehouses built by Agrippa. The **Temple of Castor and Pollux**, of which three columns still stand, was one of the largest of the period from its foundation (early fifth century BC), and retained its prestige even after being rebuilt several times. The cult of the Dioscuri, the sons of Jupiter and Leda, was imported from Greece by the aristocratic party in the early fifth century BC. Two horsemen had led the Romans to victory at the Battle of Lake Regillus against the Latins (499 BC). They were later seen watering their horses at the Juturna Spring, after announcing victory to the city, and then vanished. The Senate frequently met here and it also housed the office of weights and measures and booths used by bankers. The myth of the Dioscuri is associated with the Juturna Spring. This flowed into a monumental basin built by Aemilius Paulus, the general who conquered Greece. He also erected the statues of the two heroes set in the center of the spring, since the Dioscuri are said to have appeared a second time to announce the victory of Aemilius Paulus. To the south is the chapel of the goddess Juturna, rebuilt under Trajan.

The Temple of Antoninus and Faustina

### The East Side

The irregular complex to the north of the Temple of Vesta is the ***Regia***, the king's residence. Legend says it was once the house of the King of Rome, Numa Pompilius. Under the Republic it became the seat of the *Rex Sacrorum*, an official who replaced the king in his priestly functions, but was always rebuilt with the same plan and other features. It seems to have two parts: on the south a rectangular zone of three rooms, identified as the shrine of *Ops*, goddess of harvests, and Mars, divine ancestor of Romulus; to the north is a large arcaded court.

The **Temple of Antoninus and Faustina**, north of the Regia, survived because it was converted into the church of

The Basilica of Maxentius

San Lorenzo. Built by Antoninus Pius for his wife the deified Faustina, after his death it was also dedicated to him. It is set on a tall plinth with an altar base set in the steps. A little further to the east is a circular temple, now the vestibule of the church of Santi Cosma e Damiano: this may have been the temple dedicated to Romulus, son of Maxentius, or the Temple of Jupiter Stator, dedicated by Maxentius to his dead son and converted by Constantine into a temple for the cult of Jupiter.

The north-east zone, the hill called the Velia is dominated by the **Basilica of Maxentius**. Only the north aisle survives. Begun early in the fourth century AD on the site of the *Horrea Piperataria* (spice warehouses), it consisted of a nave borne on eight marble columns and side aisles, running east to west.

The aisles formed three areas with coffered barrel vaults. The entry was to the east, and the emperor's statue was set in the apse of the west side. This was confirmed by the discovery of a huge acrolithic statue of Constantine now in the Capitol. Then, perhaps under Constantine, the building's main axis was altered so it ran north to south: a more monumental entrance was opened facing the Forum with a portico borne on four large porphyry columns and a flight of steps. An apse was set in the far wall, lined with niches for statues. From the end of the fourth century AD it housed some of the city's most important institutions: the *Praefectura Urbi*, which replaced the consulship, and the *Secretarium Senatus* or senatorial court.

Detail of the relief set on the balustrade
of the church of San Giuseppe
ai Falegnami, which represents
Saints Peter and Paul in the prison

## The Mamertine-Tullian Prison

The tradition holds this was built by Ancus Marcius (640-616 BC) as a deterrent to criminals. It was called the Mamertine after the Sabine god Mamers (Mars), believed to have had a temple nearby. The present building is part of the original complex which extended towards the Arx, with other rooms hewn out of the volcanic stone (*latomie*). The location of the prison is significant: at triumphs, the most important prisoners, before the ascent to the Capitoline Temple of Jupiter, would be taken from the procession and thrown in the *carcer*. Jugurtha, King of Numidia, Vercingetorix, King of the Gauls, Sejanus, the minister of Tiberius, are some of the names recorded on one of two stones at the entrance to the upper cell, while the other bears a list of Christian martyrs. But there is no proof that St. Peter or St. Paul were ever held here, as traditionally believed.

Through a modern passageway we enter a chamber with a trapezoidal plan, built in the second century BC and embellished in the eighteenth with an altar with busts of Peter and Paul. This is the true *carcer*, where the prisoners were held, being lowered through a trapdoor, the only entrance. It was the most ancient and secret part, the *Tullianum*, a name derived from a spring of water (*tullus*) which rose here. It is also said to derive from King Servius Tullius, who may have built it as a cistern. Once it was circular, with walls built entirely of blocks of *peperino* stone and covered with a *tholos* (false dome). Today the ceiling has been lowered. The interior was dark and dank. An iron door conceals a sewer that flows into the Cloaca Maxima, carrying off the water that collects in the well. As if in a symbolic victory, Christian tradition holds this to be the place where St. Peter made water gush from the stone to christen the prison guards, as depicted in the bas-relief on the altar.

## Santa Maria Antiqua

The church was laid out in the first half of the sixth century AD in part of the imperial residence on the slopes

Interior of the church of Santa Maria
Antiqua

of the Palatine. When Belisarius retook Rome from the Goths, this area gave access to the hill where he established the seat of Byzantine government. The buildings erected by Domitian were converted by adapting the portico in front to a narthex dedicated to the cult of Mary. Buried in a landslide in 847, it was rediscovered in the last century and recently restored. On the right of the apse are traces of four superimposed layers of decoration. The most ancient image, *Mary as Queen of Heaven with the Christ Child and an Angel*, was painted soon after the Byzantine conquest (first half of the sixth century). The strongly Byzantine character is evident in its frontal representation and descriptive linearity. The fresco was covered with an *Annunciation* by an artist who was more refined in the use of color and effects of light. It dates from 565-578, and is the first sign of the renewal of the Hellenistic pictorial tradition. This phase was short-lived: the depictions of the *Fathers of the Church* are more conventional, dating from the age of Martin I (649-655). Pope John VII (705-707) had the arch of the apse repainted with a complex iconography in which angels adore Christ on the cross.

The other walls are also decorated with frescoes: the left aisle has a row of saints with Christ in the center, surmounted by Old Testament scenes. The frescoes in the chapel of Theodotus (left of the presbytery) represent Roman art of the eighth century under Pope Zacharias (741-782). The decoration of the chapel with the lives of Saints Quirico and Julitta is dominated by a *Crucifixion* which reveals how influences from Constantinople were being replaced by a more rapid narrative style with Oriental influences. The Oratory of the Forty Martyrs reflects the transformation of the church and the Christianization of the cult of the nymph Juturna. The apse is decorated (seventh century) with paintings that exalt the devotion of the soldiers condemned to die in the waters of a lake in Armenia during Diocletian's persecutions.

The round Temple of Vesta

### The Temple of Vesta

This building is circular like the ancient huts of Latium, with a hole in the roof to let out the smoke. It was burnt down and rebuilt many times. Its present form is due to restoration by Julia Domna, wife of Septimius Severus. The cylindrical cell is decorated with half columns, while the outer Corinthian columns rest on bases detached from the podium. The frieze was carved with cult implements (horses' tails, mirrors, olive branches, pitchers and *bucrania* or animal skulls). The cell did not contain the statue of the goddess, who was evoked by the perpetual fire, while an underground chamber contained the objects that Aeneas was said to have brought from Troy, including the Palladium, a small statue of Minerva, a pledge of the universal rule she had promised to Rome. An image of Vesta was placed in the Ionic aediculae dating from the reign of Hadrian, next to the entrance of the **House of the Vestals**. These were virgin priestesses consecrated to the cult of the goddess, chosen by the Pontifex Maximus from girls of patrician families, who served for thirty years with the duty of chastity. The Vestals lived in a kind of convent, laid out around a court surrounded by porticos. They enjoyed many privileges, but if they profaned their vow of chastity they would be buried alive and if they allowed the sacred fire to go out they were flogged.

### The Antiquarium Forense

In the cloister of the convent of Santa Romana Francesca, the archaeologist Giacomo Boni installed an Antiquarium, now being restored, to exhibit finds from the excavations in the Forum. A statue of Aesculapius from the *Lacus Iuturnae* welcomes the visitor to the entrance on the ground floor, the only part open to the public. In Rooms 1-5, containing materials from the archaic period, the original display is unaltered. Room 1 contains a model of the cemetery near the Temple of Antoninus and Faustina and reconstructions of some of the graves. Room 2 contains burials within tree trunks, dating from the most recent phase of the use of the Forum as a cemetery (mid-sixth-seventh century BC). Most of the exhibits are kept in the section still closed to the public. They include a marble head from Magna Graecia in a severe style (mid-fifth century BC) and the fragmentary group of the Dioscuri with their horses, from the Juturna Spring, dating from the second century BC. Of exceptional importance are the fragments of the late-republican marble frieze from the Basilica Aemilia, with episodes depicting the origins of Rome (construction of the wall of Lavinius, the rape of the Sabine maidens, the punishment of Tarpeia and battle scenes).

### The Arch of Titus

At the point where you climb towards the Palatine, the **Arch of Titus** owes its preservation to incorporation into the mediaeval fortifications by the Frangipane family. Its present appearance is the result of heavy-handed nineteenth century restoration, which made good the missing parts of the attic and piers. It was erected by Domitian in memory of his brother, the deified Titus (after AD 81), to celebrate his triumph in the Jewish War of AD 70-71, as shown by the dedication on the side facing the Colosseum in the attic above the single arch. The continuous frieze running round the outside represents the triumphal procession in popular style, and the archivolts have winged Victories hovering above a globe. In the center of the coffered vault of the arch is a depiction of the apotheosis of Titus, while two side panels illustrate his triumph. In the background are the *fasces* borne by lictors, the imperial quadriga or chariot, with Titus crowned by Victory, followed by personifications of the Roman People and Senate, while the goddess Rome drives the horses. The relief opposite depicts an earlier moment, with the procession about to pass through the Porta Triumphalis into the Forum Boarium. The Roman soldiers

The Arch of Titus

Arch of Titus, inside the passage
and a panel that depicts the procession
entering the Porta Triumphalis bearing
booty from Solomon's Temple

carry plunder from the Temple of Jerusalem, symbols of Judaism (the silver trumpets, Ark of the Covenant and the *menorah* or seven-branched candlestick), while the tables with handles are spread with other objects or bear the names of the cities defeated or painted episodes of the war. A historical record of exceptional importance, the arch testifies to a radical revival of Roman art through the search for a more tactile coloring, effects of light and shade, and spatial dynamism.

### The Roman Forum from the Sixth to Ninth Centuries

The appearance of the Forum seems to have remained much the same at least until the sack of Rome by the Visigoths in 410. Only after this do we hear of buildings being restored, but without altering their functions. All through the sixth century and part of the seventh the Forum retained its monumentality and prestige, but then there are records of the first changes in its appearance, with new commercial buildings and the conversion of some to churches. Far-reaching changes began in the seventh century, reflecting the political and religious climate. Workshops were installed to reuse the metal and marbles stripped from the buildings, showing that many of them were no longer considered important.

The role of the Church became increasingly dominant. In the eighth century five deaconries were created in the churches of the Forum. These were religious institutions devoted to welfare. They contained stores of grain, wells and even a small spa in the House of the Vestals. The creation of religious institutions led to an expansion of the built-up area, but it was radically altered in the second half of the ninth century by disasters like the earthquake and floods of 847. No attempt was made to clear the debris or repair the sewers, which were abandoned. The area reverted to swamp and the houses had to be built higher. Some fine residences were then added, together with craft workshops and shops.

2

# The Palatine

# The Palatine

The Palatine is closely associated with legends of the city's foundation: Aeneas reaching Latium from Troy was welcomed by King Evandrus on the Palatine; the basket containing Romulus and Remus was left by the Tiber in a cave later called the Lupercal on the slopes of the hill. The city founded by Romulus overspread the hill and Romulus himself lived in a house, identified as a hut on the south-west corner of the hill, continually restored in honor of the city's mythical founder. A village was discovered on the spot where tradition placed the hut of Romulus, enabling settlement on the site to be dated to the eighth century BC. Its elevated position close to the river made it suitable for settlement and memories of the antiquity of the site enhanced its holiness. A number of ancient traditional cults are associated with it, among them the *Lupercalia*, when wolf-priests would run about and strike married women with thongs as a fertility rite. Its sacred character led Augustus to build his palace next to the hut of Romulus. He also built the Temple of Apollo close by, so increasing the legitimacy of his *imperium* by presenting himself as the second founder of Rome. He bought the house of the orator Hortalus and extended it by purchasing neighboring houses. In late republican times the Palatine was also the residential district for much of the ruling class. Excavations have revealed their remains, largely obliterated by the imperial palaces. Tiberius was the first to plan a monumental residence, the *Domus Tiberiana*, followed by Nero (the *Domus Transitoria* and part of the *Domus Aurea*). With Domitian the emperors created the dynastic

*Domus Flavia*, octagonal fountain
of the upper peristyle

palace: a new architectural model, consisting of an enclosed complex, where the public and private quarters were separate, allowing the emperor to emerge and present himself to his subjects in a hieratic light. Subsequent extensions perfected and codified the model and the name *Palatium* was soon used to mean any palace. The last work on the Palatine was the Temple of the Sun, built by Elagabalus, the last but one of the Severians.

The Palatine formally remained the seat of empire but gradually lost its political centrality. Besides being the occasional residence of emperors and popes, it was turned into a fortress by the Frangipane in the eleventh and twelfth centuries. At the Renaissance it was again overspread with gardens, noble villas and vineyards, but this led to the plundering of its riches.

### The *Clivus Palatinus*

This gives access to the hill from its northern slopes, starting from the Arch of Titus. On the right the visitor will find a series of brick walls, the remains of an arcaded commercial structure (*Porticus Margaritaria*). Further up, a modern ramp, also on the right, leads to gardens known as the **Farnese Gardens** laid out in the sixteenth century over the *Domus Tiberiana*.

### The *Domus Tiberiana*

The first of the imperial palaces, erected by Tiberius, extended by Caligula, restored by Nero and Domitian. The arched structures facing the Roman Forum are all that remain. Of the central area, which covered almost the whole west part of the hill, we can see the substructures, over which spread the Farnese Gardens. It is conjectured that Nero's restructuring consisted of the creation of a central pavilion and others at the sides, separated by gardens, and the delimitation of this platform by the addition of a long cryptoporticus on the east side.

Southern front of the *Domus Tiberiana*,
towards the Forum

Podium of the Temple
of the *Magna Mater*

## The South-West Zone

On the west and north slopes recent excavations have revealed the remains of Iron Age huts, with elliptical bases cut into the tufa and holes for posts that once supported walls of reeds and mud and straw roofs. A little further north is a hill with a grove of holm oaks. This is the plinth of the Temple of *Magna Mater*, an Oriental goddess venerated in the form of a black stone (perhaps a meteorite), whose worship came to Rome in 204 BC, during the Second Punic War. Her temple was completed only in 191 BC. The shrine has been reliably identified through the discovery of the cult statue of the goddess. Ancient sources locate other shrines nearby. Some of them have been excavated and identified, like the Temple of Victory. Its *favissae* (sacred pits) were found to contain two splendid pottery heads of the goddess from the early third century BC. They were probably part of the decoration of the front of the temple. The antefixes with the head of Juno Sospita, dating from the early fifth century BC, must have come from the decoration of another sacred building.

## The *Domus Flavia* and *Domus Augustana*

This is a single, enormous complex built on the central part of the Palatine, obliterating earlier buildings on the site, in the late first century AD. It is divided into two areas: to the west is the *Domus Flavia*, containing the areas where state business was conducted; to the east the *Domus Augustana*, the emperor's private quarters. It was built by Domitian to an innovative project by his architect Rabirius. Despite the highly impressive remains, it is no more than a shadow of what it was: magnificent rooms lined with polychrome marble, spacious courtyards with gardens and fountains, frescoed rooms and splendid statues. We approach the *Domus Flavia* from its west side. This used to be flanked by a colonnaded portico which continued along the north side with the principal entrance from the Forum. The nucleus of this first area is an immense peristyle with an octagonal

*Domus Augustana*, view from above
of the lower peristyle and the central
fountain

*Domus Augustana*, view of the Stadium

fountain in the middle, onto which opened the rooms for state business. In the center of the north side is an immense chamber, the Royal Hall. The emperor's throne once stood in the apse at the end of the hall. Here official audiences and assemblies in honor of the emperor were held. Another apsed room lies to the west. It is described as a basilica because the interior was divided into a nave with side aisles. It may have been the emperor's council chamber. Another room, with a heated floor, opened onto the south side of the peristyle. It was the emperor's banqueting room, the *coenatio Iovis*, where the guests ate reclining on their *triclinia* (couches) and cheered by the flowing of two fountains. Some rooms below it were covered when the Flavian palace was built. The refinement of the frescoes and marbles suggest these are the remains of Nero's first residence, destroyed by the fire of AD 64 and replaced by the *Domus Aurea*.

The *Domus Augustana* extends east and is arranged on two levels. The upper one, closely linked to the *Domus Flavia*, is laid out around a spacious peristyle, with a pool in which there used to rise a small temple. The lower level (closed to the public, but it can be viewed from above) faces onto the Circus Maximus with a very scenic colonnaded exedra. The rooms are not of modest size, suggesting these were the private quarters. The court originally had two arcaded levels, with the walls probably lined with marbles, plundered over the centuries.

An integral part of the palace, at the east end of the hill, was its **Stadium**, elongated in form, with a semicircular stand for the emperor and his family in the middle of the long east side. Despite the name, it was probably a large garden with a riding track, where members of the household could stroll amid flower beds and works of art.

### The Southern Corner: The Severian Buildings

If you pass around the Stadium behind the imperial stand you come to a large artificial terrace built by Septimius

View of the Circus Maximus
and the southern slopes of the Palatine.
Model of ancient Rome. Museo
della Civiltà Romana, Rome

Severus, which extends the palace into a sloping zone. This had a platform for watching contests in the circus below. The palace baths extended between this platform and the Stadium. Built under Domitian, they were rebuilt by Septimius Severus, who also had the south corner of the hill decorated with a nymphaeum set on several levels. Called the *Septizodium*, only its foundations remain.

### The East Corner

Our visit ends by leaving the enclosed excavation site and making for the church of San Bonaventura, built in the Barberini vineyard, and the church of San Sebastiano towards the Forum. It stands in an artificial terrace, formerly occupied by an immense arcade surrounding a garden with the Temple of Elagabalus, dedicated to the Sun and to the emperor, who wished to be identified with it.

### The Circus Maximus

Today we can only see a small section of the stands, on the curved south side, but this is one of the largest places of entertainment ever built. It had an elongated rectangular plan, with the shorter sides curved and surrounded by terraces raised on several tiers of arches, which could seat over 200,000 people. Down the middle ran a low wall (the *spina*) around which the chariots raced. On the *spina* were arranged two obelisks, brought from Egypt, with seven eggs and seven bronze dolphins used for counting the laps. The structure was built and rebuilt many times. First the wooden stands were rebuilt in stone, then in the late fourth century BC the starting gates for the horses were added at the short north end. Under Augustus the first obelisk was installed. After the fire of AD 64 Nero had the stadium rebuilt to increase its capacity, and the damage caused by a fire under Domitian was repaired by Trajan. It was one of the most popular places in Rome down to at least the fourth century AD, when chariot racing peaked in popularity.

## The Farnese Gardens

To confer luster on his family, in the sixteenth century Cardinal Alessandro Farnese laid out gardens on the remains of the Palatine. The complex was planned as a series of terraces linked by flights of steps leading up to the *Teatro del Fontanone*. Its center lay in the frescoed *Casina*, surmounted by aviaries. A system of underground passages was laid out in the base of the *Domus Tiberiana*, which also served as a substructure for the gardens, decorated with ancient sculptures. The gardens passed to the Bourbon Kings of Naples and fell into decay, until travelers on the Grand Tour rediscovered the hill's romantic beauty between the seventeenth and nineteenth centuries.

## The Temple of Apollo and House of Augustus

The character of the Palatine underwent a radical change with Augustus, who established his residence on the site of *Roma Quadrata*, by the hut of Romulus, the stairs of Cacus and the Temple of Victory, associated with his military triumphs. To build it he bought up a number of houses belonging to grandees of the day. The hill was made even more sacred by the Temple of Apollo, built in 28 BC in a part of the house that was struck by lightning, hence chosen by the god. The temple was built to fulfill a vow made when praying for victory over Mark Antony at Actium (31 BC). The bare concrete core of the plinth fails to suggest the original splendor of the building, which was faced with white marble and had doors lined with gold and ivory. Archaic statues decorated the pediment, while the cult images brought from Greece were carved by the greatest sculptors of the fourth century BC. Augustus brought the Sibylline Books, containing prophecies of the future, from the Capitoline Temple of Jupiter and placed them in the pedestal of the statue of Apollo. The temple was built to a splendid Hellenistic design, laid out on two terraces, in a dominant position. It had hanging gardens and a square surrounded by a portico and decorated with statues of the fifty

*Preceding pages*
House of Augustus, Room of the Pine Festoons

House of Augustus, Room of the Masks, west wall with backdrop alluding to the satyr plays

House of Augustus, detail of the refined painted decoration of the "studiolo"

daughters of Danaus, who murdered their Egyptian husbands and were tormented in Hades by being forced to carry water in leaking pots. Excavations have recovered some statues and terracotta plaques with subjects related to the cult of Apollo. Augustus identified himself with the god as the defender of morality and social order to further his political program. The temple communicated with his private residence, being set in the wing used for state business. This consisted of spacious chambers laid out around a peristyle with elegant marble floors and splendidly decorated walls. His private apartments were plainer and more spartan. A drive separated them from those of his wife Livia. A number of rooms still preserve a fresco cycle in "Style II Advanced," such as the Room of the Masks. The walls reproduce the wooden structure of a stage, enlivened with recesses and projections, while the stage doors have curtains decorated with landscapes. To the same phase belongs the Room of the Pine Festoons, decorated with realistic pine branches set between narrow wooden pillars arranged on a high podium in front of a wall, beyond which we glimpse a portico. The room that surpasses all others in refinement and variety was the upper *cubiculum* or "studiolo." Certain details stand out against a backdrop of reds, yellows and blacks, with white architectural elements overgrown with vegetation revealing the Alexandrian origins of a great artist. It is here that Augustus concealed his secret Hellenistic "modernity," tinged with exoticism. Here he also indulged his love of reading the volumes arranged in two symmetrical libraries in the east sector, which can still be recognized after rebuilding under the Flavians. This helps explain why the name of *Domus Augustana* was applied to the Domitian palace, and the relatively small dimensions of the excavated part of the House of Augustus.

### The House of Livia

The discovery of lead piping with the inscription *Iulia Augusta* shows that Livia lived in the two-story house dating from late republican times (75-50 BC) to the north of the house of her husband Augustus. This was before the Augustan complex was rebuilt and embellished as the private apartments of the sovereign (30-20 BC). You pass through a sloping passage and enter an atrium covered by a roof and paved with a simple mosaic, a cool island before the dining room (*triclinium*) on the south-west and a reception room (*tablinum*) flanked by two wings on the south-east. The panels in "Style II Advanced" decoration have been restored to their walls. When you enter the *tablinum* you see three imaginary doors opening onto mythological scenes, while the architectural elements framing them create vistas which deceive the eye, attracted by the motifs in Egyptian style. Finally there are highly original views of small city streets. In the left wing, the panels on the upper level depict fantastic figures paired heraldically at the sides of candelabra and perched on the branches of the tree of life, the kind of eccentricities which Vitruvius at that very time condemned. The right wing has a depiction of a portico of Corinthian columns with festoons of foliage, flowers and fruit tied with ribbons, from which hang items associated with rural cults. The decoration, like that of the inner enclosure of the *Ara Pacis*, evokes a mythical Golden Age renewed under the reign of Augustus. At the top, sequences of figures, animals and ritual scenes, painted impressionistically, make this yellow frieze a fine example of landscape painting. On the floor above, some of the rooms and the original atrium still survive, together with a door facing east, which was walled up during conversion to the *Domus Augustea*.

### The Aula Isiaca

Near the Casa dei Grifi, today cut off by the foundations of the Palace of Domitian, there used to stand a late republican *domus*. All that remains is an apsed chamber with the remains of Style II paintings. The walls were detached, restored and exhibited in the Loggia Mattei, a room in the *Domus*

House of Livia, right wing, detail
of the painted decorations of rich
vegetable festoons

Aula Isiaca, detail of the pictorial decoration with Isidian and Egyptian motifs. Though classical white grounds dominate, heightening the chromatic contrasts, in the vault the artist abandoned the traditional subjects presented on the walls, indulging in an expressive freedom rare in ancient decoration. This can be clearly seen in the red ribbon interwoven with a sinuous band of blue, framed by lotus flowers and large yet delicate rose petals with curled

*Augustana*. The Aula Isiaca takes its name from its decorations, which are related to the cult of Isis (the *situla* or drinking vessel, lotus flower, solar disk and snake). They date from the period of Augustus, after his victory at Actium, when there was a vogue for using Egyptian motifs as simple decorative features. Some scholars see this as the house of Mark Antony, which passed on his death to Agrippa. Agrippa may well have also owned the villa of the Farnesina, whose paintings (now in Palazzo Massimo) can be attributed to artists who had much in common with those who painted the Aula Isiaca.

### The Loggia Mattei

Erected in the fourteenth century between the *Domus Flavia* and the Stadium was this small villa of the Stati family. In the sixth century it passed to the Mattei, who added avenues of bay trees, myrtles and cypresses. Finally the neo-Gothic Villa Mills was built over it and then demolished when excavations brought the imperial ruins to light. However, a Renaissance loggia survives, today set within a rectangular Roman hall. It has a row of three grey granite columns with sixteenth century Ionic capitals, stucco egg moldings and traces of gilding. The vault is frescoed with grotesque motifs in frames, friezes with grotesque masks, and garlands of laurel framing squares with mythical scenes. On the corbels there are aediculae with the Muses, Apollo and Athena; in the spandrels *tondi* with signs of the zodiac, while the lunettes on the walls have scenes from the story of Venus. The mythical scenes and signs of the zodiac were removed and dispersed in the mid-nineteenth century. A long-term loan of the figured scenes, today owned by the Metropolitan Museum of Art, allowed the decoration in the vault to be recomposed, the only example of Renaissance painting on the Palatine.

### The Casa dei Grifi

The imperial buildings covered the most interesting republican residence in Rome, owned by an aristocrat. Laid

edges. It is a kaleidoscope of bright hues
(blue, green, violet, yellow, pink),
rendered even more brilliant by the rich
gold highlights

Loggia Mattei, general view of the vault
after restoration

out on two floors, it was built in the second century BC. In about 120-100 BC it was decorated with an important cycle of paintings. The house (access only by reservation) takes its name from a lunette with two white stucco Gryphons in a heraldic pose facing a cluster of acanthus. You then pass through a gate and climb a staircase into the dim interior, where you find the most ancient surviving Style II paintings covering whole rooms and fragments of wall. It is the first illusionistic painting of columns seemingly projecting from a wall. There is no attempt to open out the wall with views painted in perspective, only the structure of a wall built out of blocks of stone, imitating the most refined and precious marbles: alabaster, onyx, *cipollino*, porphyry, breccia, *rosso* and *giallo antico*. Though using architectural patterns, the painting recreates the illusion of an elegant interior, enhanced by black and white mosaics framed by colored bands. One of these frames is the most ancient example in Rome of a *scutulatum*, a square laid in stones and colored marbles forming a pattern of cubes in perspective (repeating

Casa dei Grifi, lunette with Gryphons
in stucco, today only partly preserved

Casa dei Grifi, the great *cubiculum* with its walls wholly preserved. This decoration, more advanced than earlier schemes, consists of three planes with different depths. The room's fresco decorations, previously removed for preservation and displayed in the museum, were returned to their original position during the recent restoration

the motif on the podium running around the walls). While the richest stores of ancient painting have been found in the Vesuvian cities, the Casa dei Grifi, like the other frescoed residences on the Palatine, shows that the models for them spread from Rome.

### The Palatine Museums: From the Origins of Rome to Imperial Splendor

Founded in the later nineteenth century to preserve artworks from excavations on the Palatine, the museum has occupied different buildings in its checkered history. Quite recently the City's Archaeological Service decided to use premises in the convent of the Sisters of the Visitation, built in 1868 over the part of the *Domus Flavia* linking it to the *Domus Augustana*. The skillfully designed display, set on two levels, presents works from the early phases of settlement and illustrates the artistic culture of the imperial palaces. The ground floor rooms contain the original structures, such as the remains of one of two nymphaeums at the sides of the sumptuous triclinium in the *Domus Flavia* and the corner of a bath from the Neronian period. The first rooms (1-3) contain archaeological relics from the prehistoric period (Paleolithic-Bronze Age) and early historical times (tenth-seventh centuries BC). Room 4 exemplifies the sacred and religious character of the hill in archaic and republican times (sixth-first centuries BC) with items from the Temple of *Magna Mater* and the Temple of Victory or from private houses. On the upper floor, Room 5 contains symbols of ideological propaganda under Augustus, the first emperor to alter the appearance of the Palatine, in which he was followed by Nero (AD 54-68) (Room 6). Rooms 7-8 and the Gallery (Room 9) document the pictorial and sculptural decoration of the imperial residences (first-fourth centuries AD).

3

# The Valley of the Colosseum

# The Valley of the Colosseum

The valley is enclosed by hills: the Palatine, Velia (leveled in the thirties to make way for Via dell'Impero), the Fagutal, Oppian and Caelian. Narrower in ancient times, it was inhabited from the fifth-sixth centuries BC. Late in the sixth century BC the streams watering it were channeled and regular roads built. It eventually became one of the most important and populous districts, traversed by what is now Via dei Trionfi, which led to the Via Sacra and the Forum. The first setback came in AD 64, when the great fire razed the district to the ground. Nero then took over the valley and hills to build his immense palace, the *Domus Aurea*. In the middle of the valley, on the site later occupied by the Colosseum, he laid out a lake surrounded by porticos and terraces. On the Velia, on the site occupied by the Temple of Venus and Rome, there rose its enormous vestibule, with a bronze statue of Nero, later transformed into Apollo and finally the Sun God. The emperor died in AD 68 and with his *damnation memoriae* (obliteration of all traces of his reign) the buildings were never completed. The new dynasty, the Flavians, were responsible for the definitive transformation of the valley with facilities for public entertainments.

## The Colosseum

The project of the Flavians was practical, since the city lacked a permanent amphitheater, but it was also political: by returning to the people the spaces Nero had requisitioned, Vespasian and his sons hoped to win the support of

The golden light of a Roman sunset reveals the results of the careful restoration now under way

View from the Colosseum of the western
part of the valley. In the background
the Arch of Constantine and
in the foreground, interrupted by
the circular structure of the *Meta Sudans*,
some structures of the *Domus Aurea*

The valley of the Colosseum
in a photograph from c. 1880.
Private collection

the common people for the new dynasty. Vespasian began work on the Colosseum soon after coming to the throne (AD 69) and it was inaugurated by Titus in AD 80 with shows that lasted a hundred days. Construction was speeded by reusing existing structures; the cost was staggering but paid for with plunder from the Jewish Wars. Domitian completed the external orders and the structures under the arena.

Under Antoninus Pius (AD 138-161) the first repairs became necessary after a fire. Fires again damaged the amphitheater several times: the worst was in AD 217; in 222 the building was again inaugurated, but repair work took another twenty years.

After Rome was sacked by the Visigoths in 410, the Colosseum remained unused for years. Restored under Honorius I and Theodosius II in the early fifth century, it was weakened further by earthquakes. As its structure decayed, the emperors, now generally Christians, felt indifference and in some cases aversion for the bloody gladiatorial shows, which were suppressed by Valentinian III in AD 438.

In the late fourth and early fifth centuries the spoliation of the building began and continued for centuries. Through the Middle Ages and Renaissance it was treated as a quarry for building materials and in the twelfth century the Frangipane family turned part of it into a fortified palace.

Over the centuries the Colosseum also gained an aura of sanctity in memory of the martyrs described in Christian sources as being massacred during the games. In 1720 the Stations of the Cross were installed in the arena. It was only in the nineteenth century that the first excavations were carried out and there were attempts at systematic restoration. The underground structures were brought to light and brick spurs were built to buttress the structure.

The outer ring of the Colosseum is almost 60 meters high; its longer axis is 188 meters and the shorter 156.

The Colosseum, a view of what remains
today of the upper parts of the *cavea*

Around the monument was an area paved in travertine and bounded by stone pillars. The outer ring in travertine is divided into four superimposed stories. The first three have arches framed by half-columns: Tuscanic in the first story, Ionic in the second and Corinthian in the third. The fourth story is a blind attic subdivided by Corinthian pilasters into sections with square windows. Above them projected corbels in which were set the poles to support the huge awning that screened the auditorium from the sun.

Spectators entered through the ground-floor arches, each marked with a number. Some entrances were unnumbered: those on the smaller axis were for the authorities and those on the larger for the gladiators. The spectators went to their seats along fixed paths. Admission was free, but the seating was assigned on the basis of social class, dividing the spectators by rank and making the entrance and exit of the crowds more rapid.

The lowest tier was reserved for senators and had stone seating. Inscriptions on the seats still bear the names of their occupants, while the others are distinguished by epigraphs indicating social classes and ethnic groups. The second tier of seating was reserved for the equestrian order, while the common people occupied the third and fourth tiers, the last of these consisting of wooden steps. Women were also relegated to the top tier, a sign of their low social status.

Its seating capacity is still debated: on the basis of ancient sources and modern measurements, a likely estimate is some sixty thousand people. Today it is not easy to imagine the interior in ancient times. The underground structures, concealed by the wooden floor of the arena, contained cages for animals and the tackle required to install the complex scenery.

An underground passage set on the central axis ran east to the *Ludus Magnus*, while on the south side another tunnel allowed the emperor to reach the royal box.

*On pages 66-67*
The Colosseum, the interior of the building. Partial view of the *cavea* from the floor of the arena

*On pages 68-69*
In the center, the underground chambers originally hidden by the floor of the arena

The Colosseum, the service passages
under the arena

## The *Ludus Magnus* and Other Facilities

These were the largest gladiatorial barracks in Rome. Only the northern part has been brought to light. Its semi-elliptical form is like a small amphitheater. All around the *cavea* ran a portico onto which opened the cells of the gladiators. They not only exercised here but lived in a state of imprisonment. Built by Domitian and restored by Trajan, these are not the only barracks for the gladiators of the Colosseum. Three other buildings faced the square: the *Ludus Matutinus* (for gladiators who specialized in wild beast hunts), the *Ludus Dacicus* and the *Ludus Gallicus*, which took their names from the origin of the gladiators they housed, namely Dacia and Gaul. Then there were the *Castra Misenatium* or barracks for sailors from the fleet at Misenum, who raised and lowered the great awning, the *Sanitarium*, where wounded gladiators were treated, the *Spoliarium*, where bodies were taken, the *Armamentarium* (weapons store), and the *Summum Choragium* for storing stage machinery.

## The Arch of Constantine

The largest known triumphal arch stands on Via dei Trionfi and was dedicated to Constantine by the Senate and people in AD 315. It commemorates his victory over Maxentius at the Milvian Bridge and celebrate the ten years of his reign (*Decennalia*). In the Middle Ages it was absorbed into the fortress of the Frangipane, and then restored and studied from the late fifteenth century.

Following the model of the Arch of Septimius Severus, it consists of three bays supported by four Corinthian columns from the Antonine Age (AD 138-161) resting on tall decorated bases. The bays are flanked by carved Victories, geniuses of the seasons and river deities. Above the entablature are statues of Dacians from the age of Trajan. Running round all its sides is a low frieze dating from the age of Constantine with scenes from the war between Constantine and Maxentius; on

The Arch of Constantine, south front

the south front the frieze represents the siege of Verona and the battle of the Milvian Bridge. In the upper register there are four *tondi* from the age of Hadrian decorated with scenes of hunting and sacrifices. In the attic, at the sides of the inscription, are four panels from the age of Marcus Aurelius with scenes of his military campaigns, taken from a monument in its honor.

Constantine's frieze begins on the shorter west side with the army's departure from Milan, while the east side shows his triumphant entry to Rome after defeating Maxentius. The *tondi* above repeat those from the age of Hadrian but date from the time of Constantine and represent the Moon/Diana on the west side and the Sun/Apollo on the north. The two reliefs on the attic come from a frieze from the age of Trajan and depict battle scenes.

The Arch of Constantine, view of Constantine's frieze and Hadrian's *tondi* over the smaller west *fornix* (passage)

On the north front the frieze shows Constantine addressing the crowd from the *Rostra* in the Roman Forum and the distribution of largesse to the people. These two reliefs reveal the distinctive style of art in the fourth century, which influenced figurative culture in the West for many centuries. Apart from its lack of formal elegance, it totally lacks perspective and realism: it has a truly symbolic function, in which the hierarchy of the representation is the overriding consideration. Above the Constantinian frieze, in the *tondi* from the age of Hadrian, there are again scenes of hunting and sacrifices, while in the attic the four panels of Marcus Aurelius represent the arrival and departure of the emperor, the distribution of largesse and the emperor's clemency to a barbarian chief. The central bay has two more panels from Trajan's frieze: on the east is the emperor's triumphant entry to Rome and to the west a battle scene.

The scenes on the arch are numerous and varied by subject, period and style. Yet despite this, there is clearly a precise program behind their choice. They were meant to communicate as effectively as possible the emperor's message. Constantine wished to be celebrated not just as the victor, but to relate himself, in ideal continuity, to the great emperors of the second century, distinguished for good government and conquests.

### The *Meta Sudans*

This was a monumental fountain erected under Domitian. It consisted of two superimposed forms: a cylinder decorated with niches and a cone-shaped body surmounted by a sphere. The cone-shaped form recalled the pillar, or *meta*, around which the chariots turned in the Circus, while *sudans* ("sweating") suggested the water that came welling out of it. It stood at the intersection of four or five of the *regiones* of Augustus and a similar number of roads, as well as on the axis of the road taken by triumphal processions which came from the Circus Maximus before turning into

The Temple of Venus and Rome
on the high podium, seen from
the Colosseum

the Via Sacra. The fountain may have been the monumental version of one of the mythical boundary stones of the Romulean city. The sources also record that the house where Augustus was born stood near here. The unusual cone-shaped fountain has thus been explained as an allusion to the *betyl*, the aniconic symbol of Apollo, the god whom Augustus recognized as his patron.

## The Temple of Venus and Rome

On an imposing plinth on the west side of the valley of the Colosseum are the remains of the largest temple ever built in Rome. It was begun in AD 121 by Hadrian, an emperor of broad culture, literary as well as technical, whose philhellenism left its mark on a whole age. The temple was built on the spot where the vestibule of the *Domus Aurea* had stood, repeating its orientation and reusing its foundations. The colossal statue of Nero (at least 35 meters high) was moved closer to the amphitheater. The temple with its Hellenized forms stood in the middle of a large artificial plinth, supported on the longer sides by a double portico of columns at the center of which were two *propylaea*, while the shorter sides gave access to the square of the Colosseum and the Forum. Inside it had two cellae facing in opposite directions, each preceded by a vestibule. Of the cella towards the Colosseum (dedicated to Venus) there remains only the apse, while the one on the west side is much better preserved, having been incorporated into the former convent of Santa Romana Francesca. The remains visible today date back to its substantial restoration by Maxentius in AD 307, after fire destroyed the whole central part of the Forum and so enabled him to start construction of the basilica.

4

# The *Domus Aurea*

# The *Domus Aurea*

The entrance is on Via della *Domus Aurea*, which climbs up the Oppian Hill from the square of the Colosseum. Guided tours (220 meters through 32 rooms) are organized in groups of 25 and last some 45 minutes.

Nero was not the first emperor to feel the need of an official residence. Leaving aside his passion for luxury, it was a political necessity. Rome was frequently visited by foreign monarchs, many of them accustomed to living in Oriental style. But his predecessors had avoided the exaggerations of megalomania, occupying "only" the Palatine. After the fire of AD 64 Nero transformed the existing *domus* into a complex of unusual magnificence, taking advantage of the space freed by the districts it destroyed and razing whole districts spared by the flames. The grandeur of the *Domus Aurea* now became legendary, like its creators Severus and Celeres: architects and engineers capable of conceiving original variants while drawing inspiration from great maritime villas on the Gulf of Naples.

*Roma domus fiet: Veios migrate Quirites / si non et Veios occupat ista domus!* "Rome is now one huge house: Romans, migrate to the town of Veio! Unless, of course, this damned house hasn't sprawled all the way to Veio!" This celebrated satire expresses popular resentment at Nero's seizure of over 80 hectares (200 acres) of land. Some of the structures and painted decorations of the Palatine (*Domus Transitoria*) emerged during excavation of Domitian's residence, the *Domus Augustana*. Remains of the *Domus Aurea* have also

Room of Achilles at Skyros, general view of the decoration of the vault and apse

Of the few surviving portraits
of Nero, who was sentenced
to *damnatio memoriae*, the Palatine
portrait, which dates from AD 59-64,
is perhaps the most attractive, both
by its workmanship and because
it has been reliably identified:
the massive head of the Domitians,
the downy beard carved in the Greek
marble, the rather soft fleshiness
of the face and the hair combed
in the Julian-Claudian fashion.

been recovered near the Temple of Venus and Rome and around the *Meta Sudans*, where Nero's Lake (*stagnum Neronis*) lay at the bottom of the valley, the focal point of the whole complex. The part we know best is the pavilion on the Oppian Hill. After another fire in AD 104, Trajan built his baths above it and so actually preserved the only building to survive.

To build this pavilion, which stretched some 370 meters from east to west (its present length is about 240 meters), Nero was forced to cut a slice out of the hillside. On the west side a retaining wall was built, while on the north were two long cryptoporticuses to protect the rooms from damp and provide passages for use by the staff.

All that remains is the front of the complex, whose rear stretched across the summit of the hill. The pavilion facing the valley was a self-contained structure built of *opus testaceum* and laid out on two floors. The upper level ended in the ridge dating from the reign of Trajan. The two levels were once linked by scenic flights of steps. The plan was arranged in harmony with the cardinal points and is notable for a marked symmetry of its parts, with the rooms laid out around two pentagonal courtyards. All the interiors, which lacked doors, services and heating, much have been used for official functions or entertainments, in a setting of natural beauty and works of art. The rather awkward way the rooms interlock was probably due to the retention of earlier structures in the hurry to complete this huge enterprise. Certainly the front was unified and harmonious, with a portico stretching along its whole length. Light was the dominant feature of the complex: it was shed from courtyards, radial peristyles, nymphaeums or simple apertures and expertly reflected through suites of room laid out on skilfully studied optical axes. The marble cladding must have been closely adapted to these volumes, but the pictorial decorations failed to live up to this highly imaginative building. We have lost the series of large scenes

Above all the skillful interplay of light and shade suggests the complex personality of the emperor before his marked psychological degeneration in the last years of his reign

painted by the legendary Fabullus. What remains is a not particularly varied series of frescoes lacking any close relationship with the spaces. They are notable for an obsession with miniaturist detail and threadlike ornaments set against flat backdrops that generate pictorial visions dominated by a *horror vacui*. These were what Renaissance artists saw when they were rediscovered, and they felt justified in using them as an inexhaustible repertory of decorative motifs.

*Preceding pages*
*Domus Aurea*, Octagonal Room with a *lumen* in the cloister vault

*Domus Aurea*, trompe-l'œil window with a lakeside panorama enlivened with figures rapidly sketched in, an example of the evocative style recorded by Pliny as typical of the age of Nero. "People no longer like painted panels or

## From Rediscovery to Myth

Anxious to distance themselves from the oppressive legacy of Nero's absolutist conception of power, the Flavians restored these immense spaces to public use. The decay of some parts of the palace favored pillaging and the reuse of its materials. After the fire of AD 104, Trajan built his baths on Nero's structures. The extensive landfills actually preserved the "House of Gold," already stripped of its marble and artworks, which the Flavians exhibited in the Forum of Peace. The rooms became underground passages, storerooms and lodgings for the staff of the baths. Only a few rooms on the west side were saved from the landfill, later becoming the oratory of Santa Felicita. The *Domus Aurea* was rediscovered by chance in about 1480, when some inquiring souls began to venture underground. It was the first ever find of major ancient painting and was avidly explored by the great artists of the day, who blazed with excitement at the discovery and were fascinated by the bizarre decorations. They copied them by candlelight and then blazoned them across the walls of important palaces (the Farnesina, Villa Madama, the Vatican loggias and apartments). This was the origin of the "grotesque," a name derived from their original location in "grottoes." The result was a model of taste which, like the Egyptomania that followed the Napoleonic campaigns, spread across Europe.

## The Visit

The tour starts from a brick passage set in the hemicycle of Trajan' Baths. You go through long barrel-vaulted galleries where you can see the original exploratory shafts which led to the discovery of the remains of the houses obliterated to build the palace. From this point you get a view of a suite of rooms on the west side, built at the same time as the pavilion on the Palatine, since the quarter was damaged in the fire of AD 64. On the original façade, now screened by the portals of Trajan's Baths, there remain

surfaces which cram mountains into a bedroom: we are beginning to paint with marble. This was invented under the reign of Claudius, while under Nero they found a way to vary the uniformity by introducing touches of color not present on the surface of the marble"

Cryptoporticus, architectural
composition on the wall, where set
among the panels and the usual wreaths
are fantastic animals, birds, flowers
and even some Egyptianized figures like
the god Anubis

A room of the *Domus Aurea*
with in the middle the marble statue
of the Muse of choral poetry, Terpsichore,
recovered during excavations
in the post-war period. Some scholars
conjecture it formed part of a group
based on original by Praxiteles, which
the Consul Lucius Mummius brought
to Rome in 146 BC after the capture
of Corinth

Nymphaeum of Ulysses and Polyphemus

fragments of the marble base of the vaulted portico, while the interior contains the rooms with the "yellow vault," the "black vault" and "the vault of the little owls." You pass by the corner of the garden portico, an attractive peristyle now concealed, being divided by the load-bearing walls of Trajan's Baths, and so enter the eastern area, laid out around two pentagonal courtyards. We are now in the "corridor of the eagles," so called from the superb decoration in which birds of prey alternate with peacocks and other birds heraldically opposed. They form a splendid setting for the central panel depicting Ariadne abandoned by Theseus.

The seated statue of Terpsichore, the Muse of choral poetry, stands out against the deep red coloring of the walls. This is one of the rare sculptures to be preserved and reflects the plan of decoration desired by the emperor-poet. Here we are in one of the building's most interesting architectural features, the Nymphaeum of Ulysses and Polyphemus. Originally it was illuminated by eight windows and water

Nymphaeum of Ulysses and Polyphemus,
vault, detail of the central medallion
(*emblema*) with the scene of Ulysses
offering the cup of wine to the Cyclops

came cascading from the back wall and gathered in a pool. On the vault is part of a mosaic of Ulysses offering a cup of wine to a reclining Polyphemus, a scene much in vogue in nymphaeums from Julio-Claudian times by its legendary setting. The room achieves an effect of great realism because of the pumice stone used to line the ceiling, evoking the atmosphere of a sea cave with its refined lighting. We now come to the part of the east wing facing the hill. The rooms are cramped and irregular in form, being hemmed in by the wall of the *horrea* built by Claudius. After glancing into a small courtyard overlooked by the windows of the nymphaeum, we go through a room frescoed with airy architectural scenes and the passageway. This once opened out onto the lawns of the polygonal courtyard, which sloped scenically down to the *stagnum Neronis* before being covered by Trajan's landfill, while on the inside it was overlooked by the most important public rooms. The largest of these, set out on a symmetrical axis, is the room with the "golden vault." Of this wonder from the past there remain the marvelous stucco partitions on the barrel vault. The room is surrounded by a passage which contains a significant example of Style IV decoration: elegant candelabra and airy architectural forms, vistas in deep perspective, slender parapets on which perch birds, and small landscapes and still lifes.

We turn the corner and enter the long cryptoporticus or underground passage running along the back of the wing. Light once entered through the "wolf mouths" in the barrel vaulting and the window embrasures in the walls. Bearing right, you follow the side of the pentagonal courtyard, leaving a suite of rooms on the left. This brings you to an area dominated by the impressing and high original octagonal room. But first it is a good idea to go through the enfilade of rooms at the sides. The first room contains a rare example of a floor with a black and white mosaic. A few steps further brings you to one of the emblematic rooms in

Room of Hector and Andromache, vaults,
sequence of the decorative panels

Imprint of a floor in *opus sectile*

the building, the Room of Achilles at Skyros. Its walls were once faced with marble. At the far end is a deep apse surmounted by a shell. The best preserved panel depicts a famous episode from the *Iliad*: Ulysses unmasks Achilles, who is hiding from the Trojan war in the palace of Lycomedes at Skyros, where his mother Thetys had dressed him in girl's clothes and concealed him among the king's daughters. The scene is skilfully composed on different planes so as to simulate depth.

Of the five rooms forming a radial pattern, the central one contained another large nymphaeum with a waterfall. The two side rooms have cruciform plans with deep niches running into the principal barrel vault and in their turn

Room of Hector and Andromache,
side panel of the vault with the scene
of the parting of Hector and Andromache

attached to the dome of the large central chamber. This bold piece of engineering had precedents in the villas or baths of Campania and was repeated with greater splendor in the dome of the Pantheon and Hadrian's Villa. It rests on an octagon which becomes a hemisphere as it rises towards the oculus at the center. These bare walls retain a simple, pure grandeur which strikes the visitor more than the decoration, originally excessive and today fragmentary.

For a long time scholars believed this was "the room that turned like the heavens," Nero's *coenatio rotunda*. It was clearly one of the rooms used for banquets, with the *triclinia* or couches arranged in a pattern alluding to solar symbolism. Unfortunately, while the walls were no doubt faced with marbles, the dome has been stripped of its decoration. Among the many conjectures, there is a persistent theory that it had a false ceiling of wood lined with thin sheets of metal, which was made to rotate by some external mechanism. Nero loved to astonish, and this room lent itself to the most sophisticated decorations. The difficulties raised by the absence of kitchens or heating could have been overcome by using stoves and portable braziers. Dishes cooked elsewhere could be served by hundreds of slaves, while scents and fragrant petals were scattered from above. In this room, yearning for the applause of his audience, Nero would have sung his own compositions while gesturing to their protagonists, represented by the wealth of Greek statuary.

Our visit ends in the Room of Hector and Andromache, which forms a perfect pendant piece, in plan, structure and imitation of the decorative syntax, to the Room of Achilles at Skyros. Set in compartments framed with stucco work there appear splendid ornamental patterns endlessly renewed and paintings of mythical scenes. In the central panel there is a marine thiasus (procession). Of the two side panels, one depicts the meeting of Paris and Helen and the other the parting of Hector and Andromache at the Scaean Gate, one of the most moving scenes in the *Iliad*.

*Photograph Credits*
Inklink, Florence: 4-5
© Scala Group, Florence: 8, 16, 19
Archivio fotografico Soprintendenza speciale per i beni
archeologici di Roma: 10, 13, 14, 18, 20, 22, 24, 27, 28, 32,
35, 36-37, 39, 40, 48, 51, 52, 54, 55, 56, 62, 72-73, 74, 76,
80, 82, 84-85, 86, 88, 89, 90, 91, 93, 94
Archivio della Soprintendenza ai Beni Culturali
del Comune di Roma: 42-43
N. Giustozzi: 46-47, 60
Archivio Mondadori Electa, courtesy Ministero per i Beni
e le Attività Culturali: 64, 68-69
Archivio Mondadori Electa/Marco Covi: 66-67
Foto Schiavinotto, Rome: 70

This volume was printed by Mondadori Electa S.p.A.,
at Elcograf S.p.A., via Mondadori 15, Verona, in 2013